GRAPHIC DINOSAURS

PTERANODON

THE GIANT OF THE SKY

ILLUSTRATED BY TERRY RILEY AND GEOFF BALL

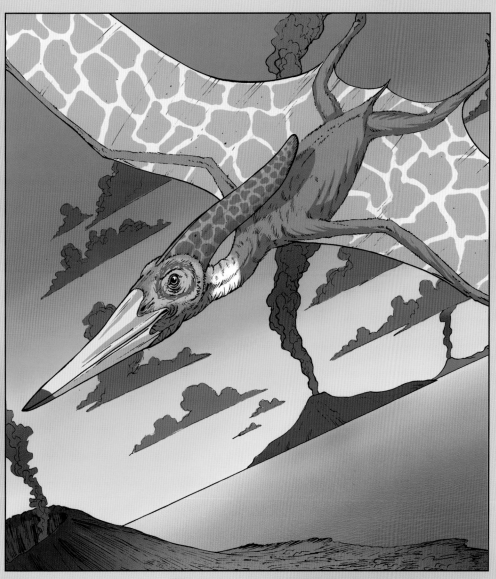

PowerKiDS
press.
New York

Published in 2008 by The Rosen Publishing Group, Inc.
29 East 21st Street, New York, NY 10010

Designed and produced by
David West Books

Designed and written by David West
Editor: Gail Bushnell
Consultant: Steve Parker, Senior Scientific Fellow, Zoological Society of London
Photographic credits: 5b, Alain Couillaud (istock); 30, Doug Rosenoff,
courtesy of Denver Museum of Nature & Science.

Library of Congress Cataloging-in-Publication Data

West, David.
Pteranodon : giant of the sky / David West.
p. cm. — (Graphic dinosaurs)
Includes index.
ISBN-13: 978-1-4042-3895-4 (library binding) ISBN-10: 1-4042-3895-6 (library binding)
ISBN-13: 978-1-4042-9625-1 (pbk.) ISBN-10: 1-4042-9625-5 (pbk.)
ISBN-13: 978-1-4042-9667-1 (6 pack) ISBN-10: 1-4042-9667-0 (6 pack)
1. Pteranodon—Juvenile literature. I. Title.
QE862.P7.W47 2008
567.918—dc22

2007011792

Manufactured in China

CONTENTS

WHAT IS A PTERANODON?

PTERANODON MEANS "WING WITHOUT TOOTH" OR "TOOTHLESS FLYER"

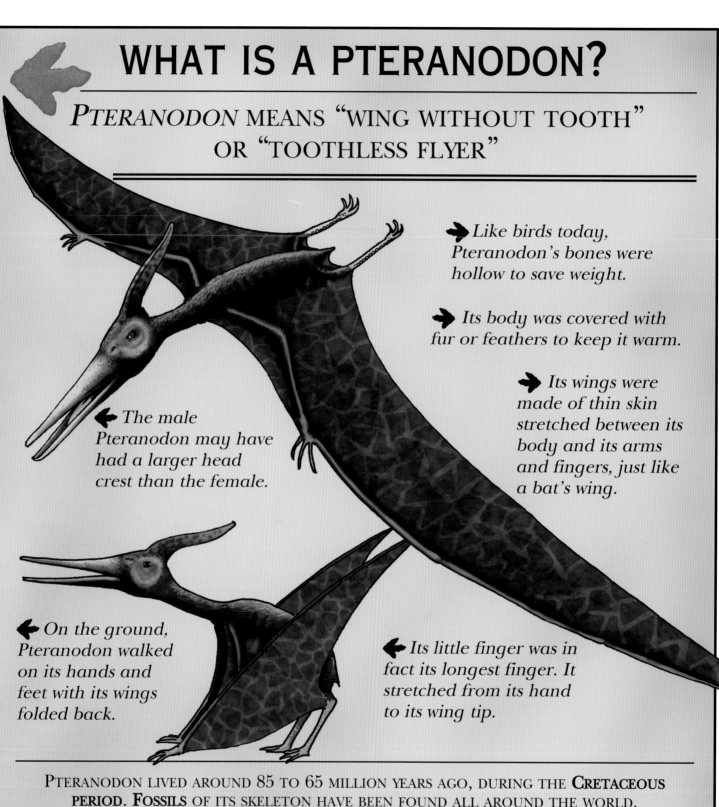

➡ *Like birds today, Pteranodon's bones were hollow to save weight.*

➡ *Its body was covered with fur or feathers to keep it warm.*

➡ *Its wings were made of thin skin stretched between its body and its arms and fingers, just like a bat's wing.*

⬅ *The male Pteranodon may have had a larger head crest than the female.*

⬅ *On the ground, Pteranodon walked on its hands and feet with its wings folded back.*

⬅ *Its little finger was in fact its longest finger. It stretched from its hand to its wing tip.*

PTERANODON LIVED AROUND 85 TO 65 MILLION YEARS AGO, DURING THE **CRETACEOUS PERIOD. FOSSILS** OF ITS SKELETON HAVE BEEN FOUND ALL AROUND THE WORLD. MANY HAVE BEEN FOUND IN NORTH AMERICA, WHERE THERE WAS ONCE A LARGE SEA.

⬅ Pteranodon had a wingspan of up to 30 feet (9 m) but it only weighed around 44 pounds (20 kg). Its head crest was up to 3 feet (90 cm) long.

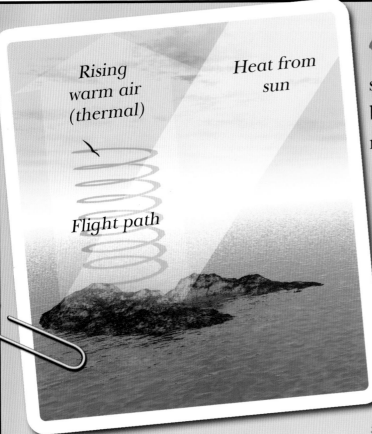

Rising warm air (thermal)

Heat from sun

Flight path

LEATHERY EGGS

Pteranodon behaved in a similar way to seabirds today. It built a nest and laid eggs, although recent discoveries have suggested that the eggs were leathery, not hard-shelled like a bird's egg. It probably cared for its young like modern seabirds as well.

FISH-EATER

Although Pteranodon could fly like a bird by flapping its wings, it spent most of its time in the air, riding the thermals to save energy. Just like seabirds, it searched for schools of fish and scooped them up as it flew just above the water's surface. Scientists think it might have had a pouch under its beak similar to a pelican's.

RIDING THE THERMALS

On sunny days parts of the sea and land get warmed up by the sun's heat. Dark areas tend to absorb more heat. The air above these areas gets warm and begins to rise. These currents of rising air are called "thermals." Large soaring birds, like albatrosses and vultures, recognize these areas. They use them to gain height by circling within the thermal. Pteranodon probably did the same.

Pelican

THEY PASS A GROUP OF PTERANODON FEEDING ON THE CARCASS OF A MOSASAURUS LYING IN THE SEA, 164 FEET (50 M) FROM THE SHORE.

SUDDENLY THERE IS PANIC IN THE HERD OF MAIASAURA. A PAIR OF ALBERTOSAURUS ARE ATTACKING.

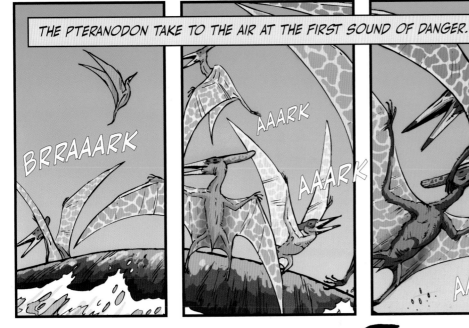

THE PTERANODON TAKE TO THE AIR AT THE FIRST SOUND OF DANGER.

AT A NEST ON THE ISLAND, A MOTHER PTERANODON PROTECTS HER EGGS.

SNAP

LIZARDS ARE NOT THE ONLY ANIMALS LOOKING FOR A FREE MEAL.

PLOP

WHEET

WHEET

ANCIENT BIRDS CALLED ICHTHYORNIS HOVER ABOVE THE NEST. THEY ARE READY TO SWOOP DOWN ON UNPROTECTED EGGS.

ONE OF THE EGGS BEGINS TO MOVE...

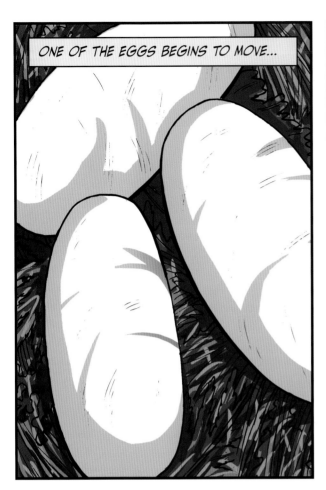

THE MOTHER NUDGES IT WITH HER BEAK AS IF TO HELP THE **HATCHLING** INSIDE.

A BEAK SUDDENLY BREAKS THROUGH, THEN THE HEAD, AS THE GASH IN THE EGG WIDENS. AFTER SEVERAL MINUTES OF STRUGGLING, THE BABY PTERANODON FINALLY BREAKS FREE.

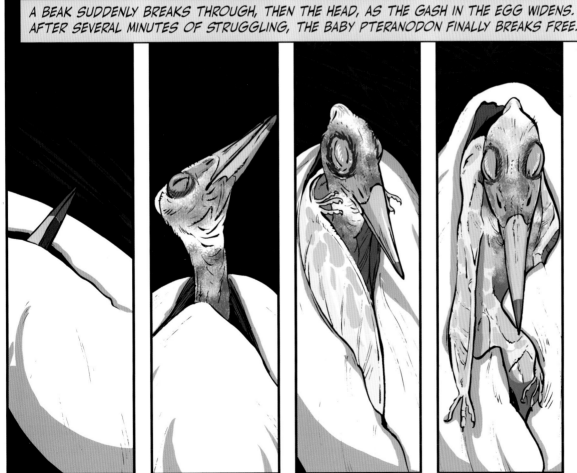

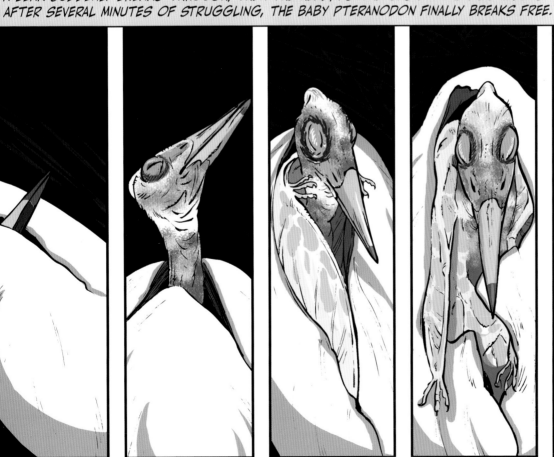

DWEEP

OTHER EGGS IN THE NEST, AND ALL OVER THE ISLAND, BEGIN TO STIR...

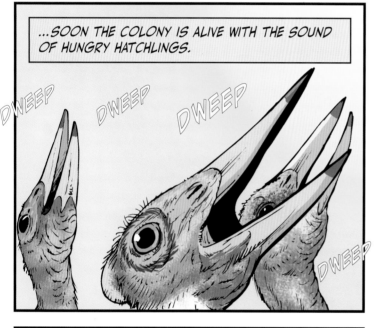

...SOON THE COLONY IS ALIVE WITH THE SOUND OF HUNGRY HATCHLINGS.

DWEEP DWEEP DWEEP DWEEP

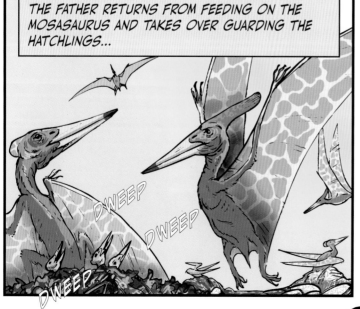

THE FATHER RETURNS FROM FEEDING ON THE MOSASAURUS AND TAKES OVER GUARDING THE HATCHLINGS...

DWEEP DWEEP DWEEP

DWEEP DWEEP DWEEP

...WHILE THE MOTHER RISES ON THE THERMAL AND CIRCLES EVER HIGHER, BEFORE HEADING OFF IN SEARCH OF FRESH FISH.

UNKNOWN TO THE FATHER, ONE OF THE HATCHLINGS FALLS OUT OF THE NEST...

...A LIZARD GRABS IT AND BEGINS TO DRAG IT AWAY.

KEEEEK

THE FATHER NOTICES AND LEAPS TO THE RESCUE. BUT THE HATCHLING IS ALREADY DEAD.

THE FATHER HAS LEFT THE NEST UNGUARDED AND A HATCHLING IS LIFTED FROM ITS NEST BY AN ICHTHYORNIS.

WHEET

KEEEEK

WHEET

THE FATHER RETURNS TO THE NEST TO PROTECT THE LAST SURVIVING HATCHLING.

AAAARK

DWEEP

DWEEP

WHEN THE MOTHER RETURNS, SHE FINDS SHE HAS ONLY ONE HUNGRY MOUTH TO FEED.

DWEEP

PART TWO... THE FIRST FLIGHT

IT IS A FEW MONTHS LATER. THE YOUNG PTERANODON IS NOW TOO BIG TO BE BOTHERED BY THE BIRDS OR THE LIZARDS. HE CAN BE LEFT ALONE WHILE BOTH PARENTS SEARCH FOR FOOD.

AAAARK

THE WATER AROUND THE ISLAND HAS FILLED WITH ELASMOSAURS. THEIR LONG NECKS RISE FROM THE SEA LIKE GIANT WORMS. A LOW-FLYING BIRD IS SNATCHED FROM THE AIR.

AAAARK

AAAARK

SOME OF THE JUVENILE PTERANODON ARE EXERCISING THEIR WINGS. THEY STRETCH THEM OUT, PREPARING FOR LIFE IN THE AIR.

A SUDDEN GUST OF WIND CATCHES THEIR WINGS AND LIFTS SOME OF THEM INTO THE AIR.

AARK

SOME OF THE JUVENILES TOPPLE OVER, BUT OTHERS KEEP THEIR BALANCE AND GENTLY FLOAT BACK TO THEIR NESTS.

AARK

AARK

A STRONGER GUST LIFTS SEVERAL JUVENILES INTO THE AIR. OUR SURVIVOR IS ONE OF THEM, AND HE KEEPS HIS BALANCE WELL. HE FEELS THE AIR RISING AND TILTS HIS WINGS TO CATCH THE THERMAL. UP AND UP HE CIRCLES. OTHER JUVENILE PTERANODON ARE FLYING WITH HIM.

AARK

AARK

AARK

BUT SOME ARE NOT SO CONFIDENT...

...AND THEY SLIDE OUT OF THE THERMAL AND GLIDE LOW OVER THE WATER.

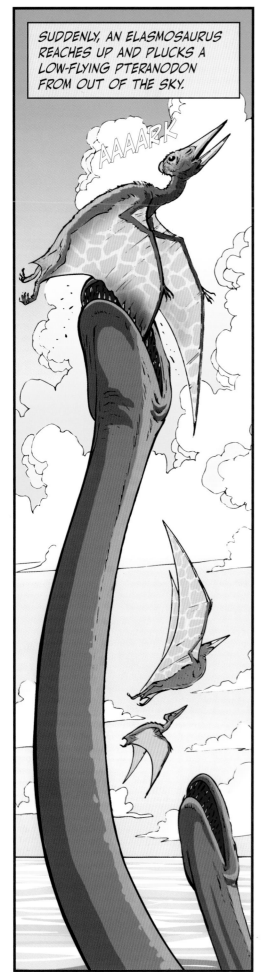

SUDDENLY, AN ELASMOSAURUS REACHES UP AND PLUCKS A LOW-FLYING PTERANODON FROM OUT OF THE SKY.

AAAARK

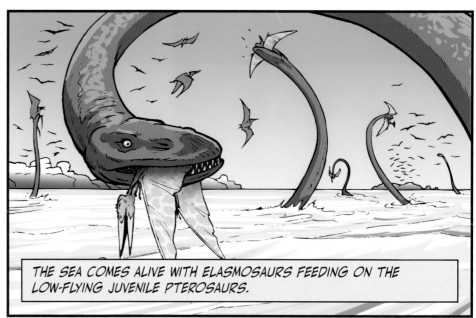

THE SEA COMES ALIVE WITH ELASMOSAURS FEEDING ON THE LOW-FLYING JUVENILE PTEROSAURS.

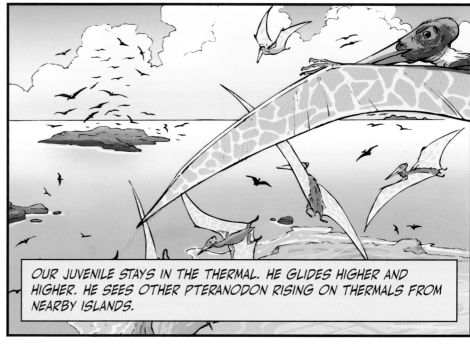

OUR JUVENILE STAYS IN THE THERMAL. HE GLIDES HIGHER AND HIGHER. HE SEES OTHER PTERANODON RISING ON THERMALS FROM NEARBY ISLANDS.

FLYING COMES NATURALLY TO THE YOUNG PTERANODON. A SPECIAL PART OF HIS BRAIN HELPS CONTROL HIS LARGE WINGS IN FLIGHT.

BY SPOTTING SUNNY PATCHES OVER THE SEA, OTHER *PTEROSAURS* AND BIRDS...

...HE LEARNS HOW TO PICK OUT THE THERMALS OF RISING WARM AIR.

ON THESE HE CAN SOAR HIGH IN THE AIR, WHERE IT IS SAFE, FOR LONG PERIODS.

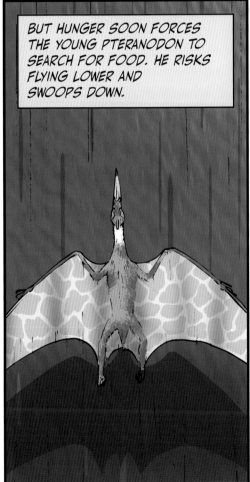

BUT HUNGER SOON FORCES THE YOUNG PTERANODON TO SEARCH FOR FOOD. HE RISKS FLYING LOWER AND SWOOPS DOWN.

HE SEES A COUPLE OF ADULT PTERANODON SKIMMING THE WATER AND CATCHING FISH.

HE JOINS THREE JUVENILES WHO HAVE SPIED A LARGE SCHOOL OF FISH.

FLYING JUST ABOVE THE WAVES IS TRICKY FOR THE JUVENILES. THEY COPY THE ADULTS AND DIP THEIR LOWER BEAKS IN THE WATER...

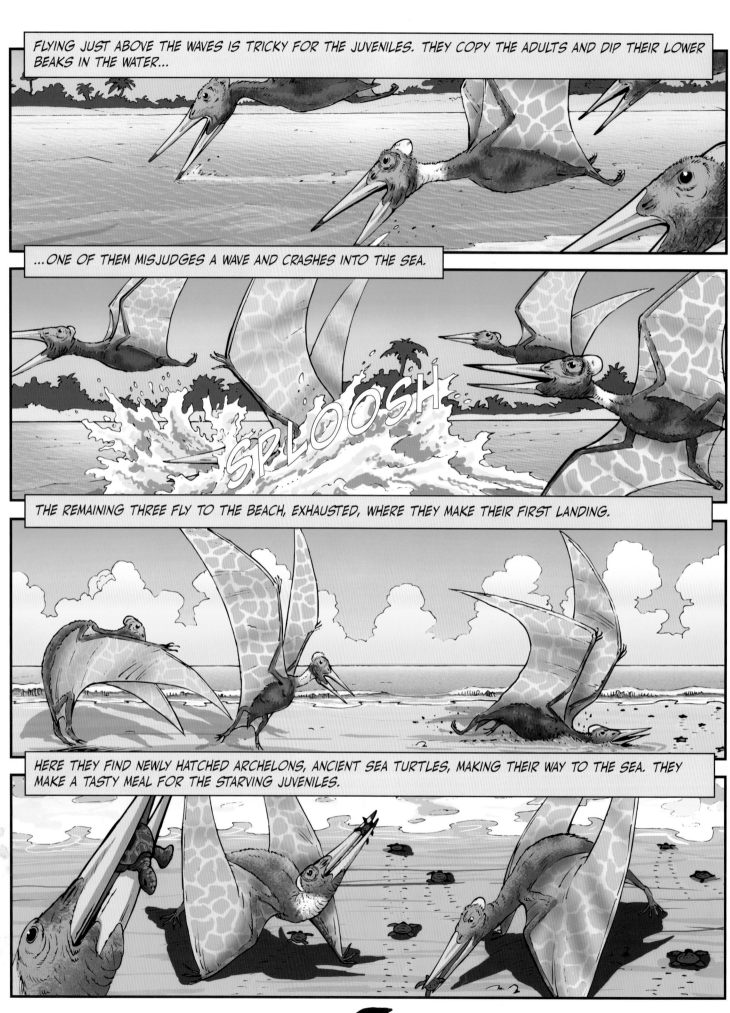

...ONE OF THEM MISJUDGES A WAVE AND CRASHES INTO THE SEA.

SPLOOSH

THE REMAINING THREE FLY TO THE BEACH, EXHAUSTED, WHERE THEY MAKE THEIR FIRST LANDING.

HERE THEY FIND NEWLY HATCHED ARCHELONS, ANCIENT SEA TURTLES, MAKING THEIR WAY TO THE SEA. THEY MAKE A TASTY MEAL FOR THE STARVING JUVENILES.

BUT THE BEACH IS NOT A SAFE PLACE LIKE THE ISLAND. A PTERANODON SQUAWKS A WARNING.

AAARK

A GROUP OF DROMAEOSAURS ARE CHARGING DOWN THE BEACH.

THE JUVENILES MAKE IT INTO THE AIR...

AAARK

AAARK

...JUST IN TIME.

AAARK

GNAARR

AS EVENING APPROACHES, THEY HEAD FOR THE SAFETY OF A SMALL ISLAND TO SPEND THE NIGHT.

PART THREE

THE STORM

AFTER SURVIVING ON SCRAPS ALONG THE SHORELINE FOR SEVERAL DAYS, OUR PTERANODON AND THE OTHER TWO JUVENILES HAVE FINALLY LEARNED HOW TO CATCH FISH.

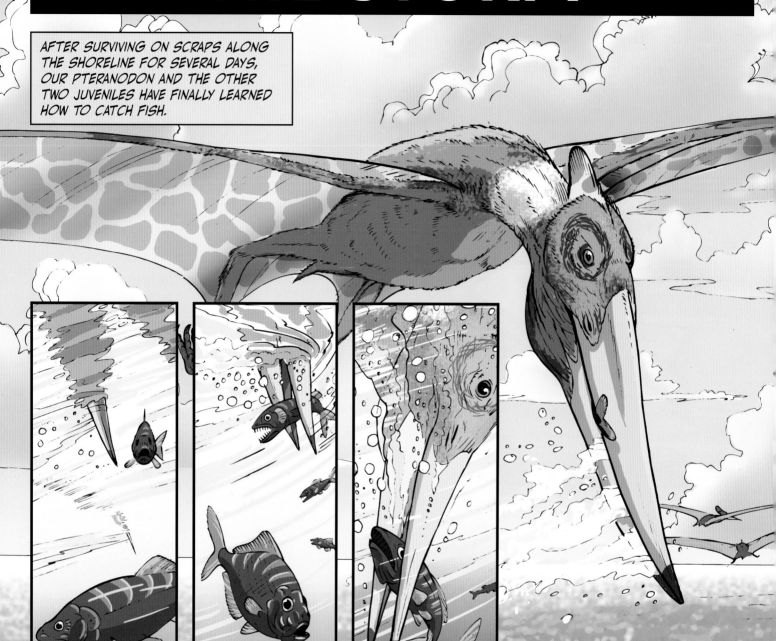

FLYING SLOWLY INTO THE WIND, HE DRAGS HIS LOWER BEAK IN THE WATER.

WHEN HE FEELS A FISH HIT THE LOWER BEAK, HE SNAPS DOWN WITH HIS UPPER BEAK.

HE THEN DROPS HIS HEAD TO TAKE THE IMPACT...

...THEN HE LIFTS UP HIS HEAD, HOLDING THE CATCH IN THE EXPANDING BEAK POUCH.

ONE OF THE OTHER TWO JUVENILES HAS CAUGHT A FISH, AND THEY BOTH FLY OFF TO A ROCKY OUTCROP TO SWALLOW THEIR CATCH.

SUDDENLY, A MOSASAURUS LEAPS FROM THE OCEAN, CATCHING ONE OF THE JUVENILES IN ITS JAWS.

AS IT CRASHES BACK DOWN IT CREATES A MASSIVE SPLASH, WHICH KNOCKS OUR PTERANODON INTO THE WATER.

KERSPLOOSH

AAARK

19

OUR PTERANODON CANNOT TAKE OFF FROM THE SEA. HIS WINGSPAN IS TOO BIG...

...AND HIS STRUGGLING ATTRACTS THE MOSASAURUS.

IT LAUNCHES ITSELF AT THE PANIC-STRICKEN PTERANODON AND MISSES. HE IS KNOCKED INTO THE AIR...

KERSPLOOSH

...A GUST OF WIND CATCHES HIS WINGS LIKE A KITE AND LIFTS HIM HIGHER...

...HE HAS ESCAPED!

BUT HE IS NOT OUT OF DANGER. THAT SUDDEN GUST OF WIND IS THE BEGINNING OF A STORM WHICH HAS QUICKLY BUILT UP OVER THE SEA.

THE SKY SUDDENLY TURNS DARK. LIGHTNING CRACKLES AROUND THE TWO PTERANODON.

DRIVING RAIN AND GUSTING WINDS BUFFET THEM AND THREATEN TO SEND THEM HURTLING INTO THE SEA.

AS THEY FIGHT TO STAY IN THE AIR, THE TWO PTEROSAURS BECOME SEPARATED.

WEAK AND TIRED, OUR PTERANODON IS THROWN DOWNWARD BY A STRONG GUST OF WIND AND KNOCKED OUT.

CRAAASH

HE AWAKENS TO FIND THAT HE IS TANGLED IN THE BRANCHES OF A TREE AT THE EDGE OF A CLIFF. THE STORM HAS PASSED AND HE HAS BEEN BLOWN FAR INLAND.

EVEN WORSE, THERE IS A YOUNG TYRANNOSAURUS FEEDING ON A CARCASS BELOW HIM.

THE PTERANODON STRUGGLES TO FREE HIMSELF AND FALLS, LANDING ON THE TYRANNOSAURUS.

GUURGH

YAAARK

AS HE FALLS TO THE GROUND, THE PTERANODON STARTS FLAPPING HIS WINGS.

GNARR

YAAARK

THE TYRANNOSAURUS ATTACKS, BUT ONLY SUCCEEDS IN KNOCKING THE PTERANODON OVER THE CLIFF.

ROOOAR

YAAARK

HE TWISTS IN MIDAIR AND SPREADS HIS WINGS. IT IS A LUCKY ESCAPE.

A SHADOW SUDDENLY RACES OVER HIM. IT IS A QUETZALCOATLUS, A GIANT PTEROSAUR...

...BUT IT IS NO THREAT TO THE PTERANODON. IT IS INTENT ON FEEDING ON THE DESERTED CARCASS.

AS THE PTERANODON PATIENTLY CIRCLES HIGHER, HE SPIES THE GLINT OF THE SEA IN THE DISTANCE.

PART FOUR

THE RETURN

IT IS A FEW YEARS LATER. THE PTERANODON IS NOW AN ADULT. HE HAS A 30-FOOT (9 M) WINGSPAN AND A LARGE CREST THAT IS BEGINNING TO COLOR.

THE EARLY-MORNING SUN MAKES THE DUST-FILLED SKY GLOW WITH REDS AND ORANGES. SMOKE FROM DISTANT VOLCANOES RISES IN COLUMNS.

IN THREE YEARS THE PTERANODON HAS TRAVELED MANY THOUSANDS OF MILES (KM) ACROSS THE SHALLOW SEA, FAR FROM HIS BIRTHPLACE...

...BUT NOW HE FEELS A NATURAL URGE TO RETURN TO THE ISLAND WHERE HE WAS BORN.

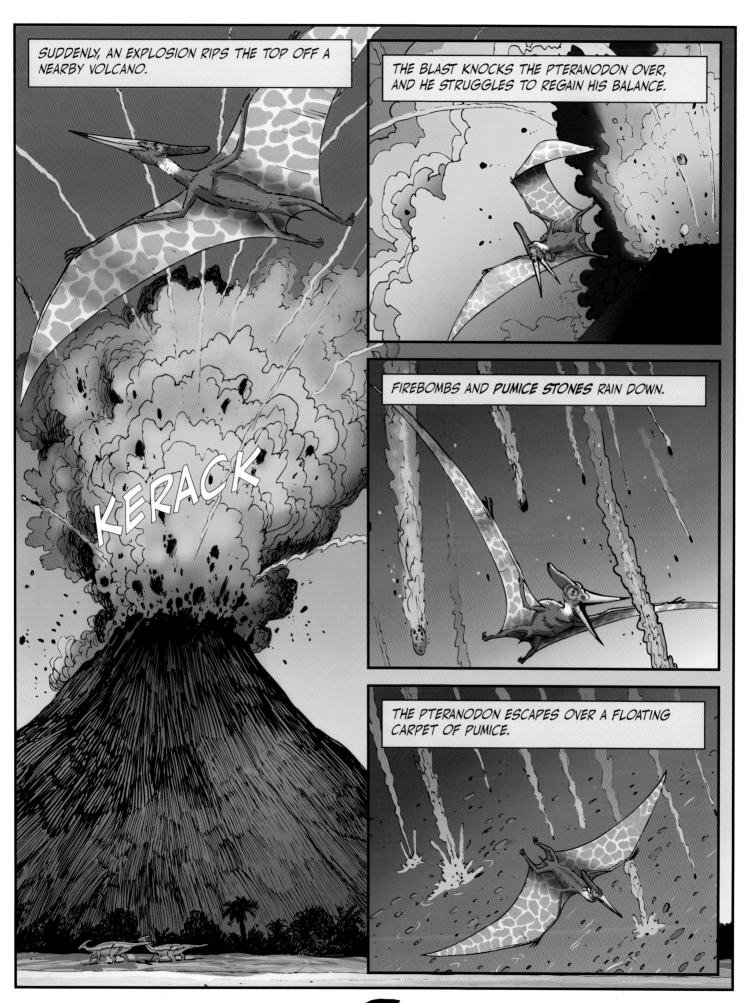

SUDDENLY, AN EXPLOSION RIPS THE TOP OFF A NEARBY VOLCANO.

KERACK

THE BLAST KNOCKS THE PTERANODON OVER, AND HE STRUGGLES TO REGAIN HIS BALANCE.

FIREBOMBS AND PUMICE STONES RAIN DOWN.

THE PTERANODON ESCAPES OVER A FLOATING CARPET OF PUMICE.

THE PTERANODON HAS NOT BEEN SERIOUSLY HURT. THAT EVENING HE PERCHES ON THE BACKBONE OF AN ELASMOSAUR'S SKELETON THAT LIES A SHORT DISTANCE FROM THE BEACH. HE WATCHES A GROUP OF YOUNG DIDELPHODON PLAYING ON THE BEACH IN THE EVENING SUN.

NEARBY, IN THE WATER, A FEW HESPERORNIS ARE SWIMMING BACK TO THEIR NESTS.

THERE IS A SUDDEN SPLASH AS A XIPHACTINUS LEAPS OUT OF THE WATER AND GRABS A BIRD.

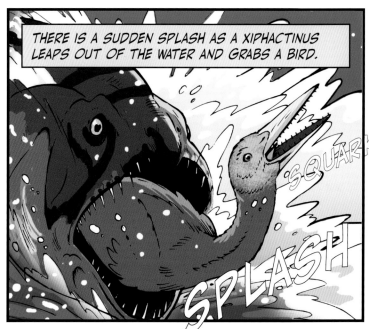

SQUARK

SPLASH

AS THEY CANNOT FLY, THE REMAINING HESPERORNIS DIVE UNDERWATER TO ESCAPE.

THE LIGHT FADES AND THE STARS COME OUT. THE SURFACE OF THE WATER RIPPLES NEARBY...

...IT IS AN ARCHELON, AN ANCIENT TURTLE.

SHE SLOWLY DRAGS HER HUGE BODY UP THE BEACH. SHE HAS COME TO DIG A HOLE AND LAY HER EGGS.

IT IS NEARLY DAWN WHEN SHE MAKES HER WAY BACK TO THE SEA.

THE PTERANODON IS WELL RESTED BY THE TIME THE SUN RISES. AS THE BREEZE GETS UP, HE TAKES OFF TO CONTINUE HIS JOURNEY HOME.

THE PTERANODON GLIDES ALONG ON RISING THERMALS. HE HAS BEEN TRAVELING FOR TWO WEEKS, STOPPING ONLY TO REST. TODAY, HE SEES FLOCKS OF ICHTHYORNIS FLYING IN THE SAME DIRECTION.

IT IS SOON MIDDAY. HIS KEEN EYESIGHT PICKS OUT SPECKS IN THE DISTANCE. AS THEY GET CLOSER HE RECOGNIZES THEIR SHAPE...

...THEY ARE OTHER PTERANODON.

SOON THE SKY IS FULL OF THEM. LIKE HIM, THEY HAVE RETURNED TO THE ISLANDS TO BREED.

THE PTERANODON RECOGNIZES HIS ISLAND AND LANDS AMONG THE MALES WHO ARE COMPETING FOR A FEMALE.

HE JOINS IN, FLASHING HIS COLORFUL CREST. SOON HE WILL ATTRACT A FEMALE WHO WILL LAY EGGS. WHEN THE YOUNG HAVE HATCHED AND FLOWN THE NEST, HE WILL SET OFF AGAIN ON HIS LONELY TRAVELS. BUT ONCE EVERY YEAR, FOR THE REST OF HIS LIFE, HE WILL RETURN TO THE ISLAND TO BREED.

FOSSIL EVIDENCE

WE HAVE A GOOD IDEA WHAT PTEROSAURS MAY HAVE LOOKED LIKE FROM STUDYING THEIR FOSSIL REMAINS. FOSSILS ARE FORMED WHEN THE HARD PARTS OF AN ANIMAL OR PLANT BECOME BURIED AND THEN TURN TO ROCK OVER MILLIONS OF YEARS.

Many Pteranodon fossils have been found in layers of rock that had been the floor of an ancient sea. One fossil had fish bones in the stomach, which suggests they spent their lives flying above the sea, catching fish like modern seabirds.

In 2004 a fossilized egg was found in China with a fossilized embryo pterosaur inside. The egg had the same volume as a chicken's egg, but its shell seemed to be made of a leathery material.

Scientists have even managed to scan the brain cavity of fossilized pterosaurs. The results showed that their brains had enlarged areas for controlling their huge wings. This suggests that they were good fliers.

Fossils have shown signs of blood vessels in the large head crest of Pteranodon. Scientists think that the crest might have been used like a car's radiator, to keep it cool, and as a display to attract a female when mating.

ANIMAL GALLERY

ALL THESE ANIMALS APPEAR IN THE STORY.

Ichthyornis
"Fish bird"
Length: 8 in (20 cm)
A seabird with a toothed beak.

Hesperornis
"Western bird"
Length: 5 ft (1.5 m)
A large, flightless seabird.

Didelphodon
"Two womb teeth"
Length: 3 ft (1 m)
A small meat-eating mammal.

Xiphactinus
"Sword ray"
Length: 20 ft (6 m)
A swift, **predatory** fish.

Archelon
"Old turtle"
Length: 13 ft (4 m)
A large, ancient turtle.

Dromaeosaurus
"Running lizard"
Length: 6 ft (1.8 m)
A small, fast-running raptor.

Elasmosaurus
"Thin-plated lizard"
Length: 46 ft (14 m)
A long-necked sea reptile.

Mosasaurus
"Meuse lizard"
Length: 49 ft (15 m)
A large, predatory sea reptile.

Quetzalcoatlus
Named after an Aztec god
Wingspan: 39 ft (12 m)
The biggest known pterosaur.

Maiasaura
"Good mother lizard"
Length: 30 ft (9 m)
A large, plant-eating dinosaur.

Tyrannosaurus
"Tyrant lizard"
Length: 39 ft (12 m)
A huge, meat-eating dinosaur.

Albertosaurus
"Alberta lizard"
Length: 30 ft (9 m)
A large, meat-eating dinosaur.

GLOSSARY

colony (KAH-luh-nee) A group of animals that live together.

Cretaceous period (krih-TAY-shus PIR-ee-ud) The time between 146 million and 65 million years ago.

fossils (FAH-sulz) The remains of living things that have turned to rock.

hatchlings (HACH-lingz) Young animals that have hatched from eggs.

juvenile (JOO-vuh-ny-uhl) A young animal that is not fully grown.

predatory (PREH-duh-tor-ee) An animal that hunts other animals for food is a predator or can be said to be predatory.

pterosaur (TER-uh-sor) The general name for a flying reptile, which means "winged lizard."

pumice stone (PUH-mus STOHN) A light rock that is thrown from volcanoes. It is so light that it floats on water.

INDEX

Web Sites
Due to the changing nature of Internet links, the Rosen Publishing Group, Inc., has developed an online list of Web sites related to the subject of this book. This site is updated regularly. Please use this link to access the list:
www.powerkidslinks.com/gdino/pter/